Hawai'i's
BEAUTIFUL
Trees

*I*n the time before human memory, a chain of massive volcanoes heaved molten, embryonic stone to the surface of the Pacific Ocean and formed an arch of bleak, rugged islands. Seeds and spores of tropical plants, borne on the breath of air currents, in the down of seabirds, or rocked adrift on the ocean swell, were among the first forms of life to arrive. They struggled to adapt to the hostile environment on the world's most isolated land mass, the Hawaiian archipelago. Many made the journey, bridging the vast distances to our islands, but perished soon after reaching landfall.

Eighty-nine percent of the native flora that evolved here in Hawai'i are unique to these islands, each species metamorphosing to survive. Protected from predators by inauspicious surroundings, tiny sprouts flourished in empty lava niches. Over time, vegetation draped these desert-like islands and majestic trees dominated the landscape.

When the first Polynesians landed, they brought with them 27 new plant species, introducing the bamboo, breadfruit, *kukui* nut trees, bananas, and coconuts that eventually transformed the original native setting.

The arrival of Westerners dramatically increased the frequency and variety of foreign species. Today, with worldwide jet service, plants from remote corners of the globe arrive and escape into the virgin forests, devastating the indigenous growth. The majority of the trees seen in the populated lowlands are primarily recent introductions. However, appreciation of the unique, endemic trees is increasing and more native trees are being cultivated.

Hawai'i is an absolute paradise for tropical plants. Our mild climate is a haven for many types of trees. Nothing compares with the relaxed protection of sitting in the shade of a grand tree that has sheltered several generations of our human family.

Library of Congress Catalog Card
Number: 96-76821
ISBN 1-56647-122-2

First Printing, March 1997
1 2 3 4 5 6 7 8 9

Printed in Hong Kong

Design by Angela Wu-Ki

Mutual Publishing
1127 11th Avenue, Mezz B
Honolulu, Hawaii 96816
Ph (808)732-1709
Fax (808)734-4094
Email mutual@lava.net

MUTUAL PUBLISHING

TABLE OF CONTENTS

HERITAGE TREES

The Heritage Tree classification used here is an artificial grouping that includes native endemic and indigenous flora, in addition to early Polynesian and Western introductions that have a long historic connection to Hawai'i. Long before man set foot on these islands, the barren lavas were slowly colonized by pioneering plant species. These naturally dispersed plants adapted and changed until 89 percent evolved into unique types found nowhere else in the world—these are Hawai'i's endemic species. The colonization and evolution of the endemic flora is an epic story that continues to be unraveled by researchers of botanical biodiversity and ecology. Those species occurring in Hawai'i naturally, but also found in other places, are known as indigenous species. The Polynesian migrations began man's plant introductions into these islands. Once Captain Cook opened the door to the West, large plant importations started that continue to this day. Anyone wishing to see endemic species faces an increasingly difficult task, since the history of Hawai'i is one of ecological disaster resulting in endemic species extinction or endangerment. The casual observer looking over a landscape lush with alien and exotic species rarely knows that Hawai'i holds the world record for greatest number of extinctions.

NATIVE WHITE HIBISCUS

Hibiscus arnottianus
Koki'o ke'oke'o

With twisted, sinuous branches draped in mosses, *Hibiscus arnottianus* makes a majestic statement in the rain forest habitat of the mountains. It is a medium tree, growing to a height of 30 feet, that adapts nicely to the lowlands, but it never assumes the sensuous form of the wild populations. The large white flowers punctuate the fresh green foliage and scent the breeze with their subtle fragrance.

OHIA LEHUA

Metrosideros polymorpha
Yellow: Lehua mamo
White: Lehua puakea
or ʻOhiaʻa kea
ʻOhiʻa lehua

ʻOhiʻa lehua is the most abundant native Hawaiian tree and occurs in forests from sea level to 9,000 feet in elevation. The specific name *poly-morpha,* or "many forms," alludes to the extremely variable nature of this plant, which can be found as dwarfs only 3 inches high or as grand denizens 100 feet tall. The genus *Metrosideros* means "heart of iron" and fittingly describes the durable, dense, and dark heartwood. Many *ʻohiʻa* trees germinate on native tree ferns and later strangle their hosts. Eventually the fern stumps rot and the tree appears to have stilt roots. The flowers provide nectar for native birds and range in color from white, yellow, and salmon to orange and red. Hawaiians believe that picking an *ʻohiʻa* flower on the way to the mountains will cause rain. *Lehua* flowers are sacred to Pele, goddess of the volcano, and, if she is displeased, the rain will obscure the path off the mountain.

KOU
Cordia subcordata

Kou is a medium tree growing to about 30 feet tall, with a dense crown of leaves that makes it a great shade tree in the hot, coastal areas where it thrives. The bright orange, scentless flowers bloom in clusters throughout the year, increasing the popularity of this stately tree. It was highly prized by the Hawaiians and was introduced by their Polynesian ancestors during their immigrations. *Kou* wood was used to fashion cups and bowls of extraordinary beauty and utility. Fallen leaves were also used to dye bark cloth (tapa) a warm brown tone.

CANDLENUT TREE
Aleurites moluccana
Kukui

Kukui is the official State tree of Hawai'i, and the tall, meandering branches present a noble stature up to 100 feet. It forms a major component of the lower mountain forests, where it is easily distinguished by its pale-green foliage. The small white flowers are borne in large clusters which are often woven with the leaves to create leis representing the island of Moloka'i. Native Hawaiians used the plant for dyes, fuel, medicine, food, oil, gum, wood, and ornamentation. It was one of the primary introductions that the first Polynesian voyagers brought to Hawai'i. The traditional uses of the *kukui* continue today, and visitors and residents proudly wear leis of polished black, brown, and white *kukui* nuts.

KOA
Acacia koa

Koa is the premier timber tree of Hawai'i. Endemic to the Islands, the largest trees were sought by the Hawaiians as the preferred choice of wood for their canoes. The largest recorded canoe was a massive 120 feet long by 9 feet deep. Although wood was the primary commodity of the tree, dyes were produced from the bark and medicine extracted from the leaves. Originally, large tracts of forests covered our mid-elevation slopes, with *koa* being the second most abundant native tree after *'ohi'a lehua*. *Koa* seedlings have fern-like foliage which change to the sickle-shaped "leaves" of the mature trees. The adult leaf is not a true leaf, but an expanded leaf stalk called a phyllode. *Koa* is thought to be of ancient lineage in the Hawaiian Islands because 50 species of endemic insects have evolved specifically for this tree. No other endemic plant hosts a greater number. Many native birds also depended on the *koa* forests, but all are either extinct or severely endangered. Today, *koa* trees are in decline but the demand for its wood is unsurpassed. Because *koa* evolved here with a community of plants and animals currently under stress, plantations and forestry plans have not been very successful. Although *koa* wood is of exceptional quality, the most beautiful way to experience *koa* is to passively enjoy the gnarled giants growing undisturbed in the remaining stands. Kupulupulu, the god of the *koa* forest, would be pleased.

BANANA
Musa paradisica
Mai'a

Bananas are perennial herbs that attain tree-like proportions to 30 feet tall. The trunks of bananas are actually the tightly bound leaf bases that grow out of an underground corm. The Hawaiian people cultivated about 50 types of *mai'a*, an early Polynesian introduction. Planting bananas by separating side shoots was highly developed in Hawai'i, with special care taken to determine moon phases, time of day to plant, soil depth, rainfall, and location of plot. Subtle dif-ferences determined the quality, texture, and quantity of fruit. In addition to food, bananas were used for medicines, fibers, religious practices, wrappings, and dyes, and the trunks were even used as rollers for canoes. Today, bananas continue to be an important agri-cultural crop grown primarily for local consumption.

LOULU PALM
Pritchardia spp.
Loulu

Loulu is the Hawaiian name for several endemic species of the genus *Pritchardia*. They hold their palmate or fan-shaped fronds proudly in rosettes crowning light-colored trunks. They can grow in the lowlands, but most of the native species are found at higher elevations, often on steep slopes or cliffs. The majority of the cultivated Pritchardias are the Fijian species, which closely resemble the endemic types to the lay person. The leaves formerly were used for thatch and plaiting, and the immature fruits eaten. The *loulu* is the only palm native to Hawai'i. Coconuts are an early Polynesian introduction whose true origins are obscured by time.

COCONUT PALM
Cocos nucifera
Niu

If one tree were to be chosen to symbolize Hawai'i to the world, the winner would be the coconut palm. The romantic vision of swaying coconut palms has been a primary lure attracting visitors to the Islands. The coconut was an early Polynesian introduction that provided fiber, timber, nourishment, drink, shelter, and ornament. The utility of this palm was so great, the Polynesians considered it a gift of the gods. No other tree could sustain life as completely as this palm. In ancient Hawai'i, the potential uses of this palm was not developed as fully as other island cultures, since taro was the staple food and other fibers and woods were preferred over the coconut. The earliest Polynesian pioneers to Hawai'i probably depended on the coconut for their survival until the material culture developed and other substitutes were found. Today, the origins of the coconut are obscured by time, but the importance of the tree is emphasized by its current pan-tropical distribution. The economic importance of the coconut is now dominated by the millions of tons of expressed oils that are used in a multitude of processed products such as cooking oil, candles, soaps, shampoos, tanning lotions, and margarine. However, for the visitor to our islands, the silhouette of coconut trees along the beach at sunset is a priceless memory that they will retain of Hawai'i.

KIAWE
Prosopis pallida

Kiawe dominates the dry lowlands of Hawai'i to such an extent that it is easy to believe that this tree is an original native species. The amazing fact is that all the trees of this species are descended from a single tree planted in 1828. The first seed was carried to O'ahu from Paris by Father Bachelot and planted on the grounds of the Catholic Mission on Fort Street. *Kiawe* is native to Peru, Colombia, and Equador and was introduced to the Royal Gardens in Paris, where Bachelot obtained the seed. *Kiawe* pods are a valuable cattle food and the seeds, which pass unharmed through the digestive tract, are aided in their dispersal. The hardwood produces an excellent charcoal and is sometimes used to create small articles. Older trees make beautiful landscape specimens, as their furrowed trunks and sinuous branches are quite sculptural.

SCREWPINE
Pandanus tectorius
Hala

Hala trees have both male and female forms. The males have a dense hardwood and drooping, white flower bracts that resemble limp dish rags. The soft, fibrous wood and pineapple-like fruits distinguish the female trees. Both sexes grow long stilt or prop roots. This was a most important tree to the Hawaiians and other peoples of the Pacific. Canoe sails, baskets, mats, and sandals are but a few of the articles plaited from *lau hala*, the dried leaves of *hala*. The fruit segments also made unique leis. It was widely believed that *hala* was an early Polynesian introduction to Hawai'i. Fossil evidence, found on Kaua'i and now being examined, could prove that *hala* dispersed here naturally. It may be proven that *hala* is an indigenous plant; however, its importance to the Polynesians was so great that they most likely carried seeds or plants on their voyages to Hawai'i.

SANDALWOOD
Santalum paniculatum
'Iliahi

Sandalwood has long been a very desirable hardwood that has led to its extensive exploitation. The Bible records the extermination of Lebanese sandalwood by King Solomon. Various species of sandalwood occur in areas of Asia, Australia, and the Pacific regions, and it is eagerly sought wherever it grows. Between 1790 and 1840, the endemic sandalwoods of Hawai'i were exploited heavily until the trade collapsed due to the lack of trees. *'Iliahi* grows extremely slowly and large trees are very rare today. There are about four endemic species in this variable group of hemiparasitic trees. As seedlings, specialized roots grow and attach to other plant roots to supplement the sandalwood's nourishment. The plants range in size from small shrubs to trees about 60 feet tall. All have the fragrant wood that fueled the greed supporting the sandalwood trade.

HAU
Hibiscus tiliaceus
Hau

It is unknown if *hau* is indigenous or a Polynesian introduction. Certainly it could have arrived by drifting in the ocean, since plants grow in saltwater and seeds remain viable for several months. Large, tangled thickets of *hau* grow in coastal areas or in valleys near streams or wet seepage zones. The Hawaiian people used the inner bark extensively for fiber, and the light wood was utilized for floats and canoe outriggers. Fires were started with soft *hau* and a hardwood stick rubbed together until friction created an ember. Medicines were made from both the bark and the flowers. The flowers last but a day—opening yellow, turning orange in the afternoon, and withering a dark orange in the evening.

MILO
Thespesia populnea

Milo is a common tree in coastal areas and may be indigenous or a Polynesian introduction. Hawaiians used *milo* primarily for bowls, and its popularity was second only to *kou* wood. Tanin, dye, medicines, oil, and fiber were extracted from the trees. The large, heart-shaped leaves provide a welcome shade in the hot coastal areas in which *milo* thrives.

SOAPBERRY TREE

SOAPBERRY TREE

Sapindus saponaria
Manele, A'e

The native soapberry trees can reach a majestic height of 80 feet. Soapberry gets its name from the fruit pulp that contains saponin, which foams and lathers with water. The Latin name *Sapindus* translates into "Indian soap." The Hawaiians used the soapy fruits, made leis from the dark black seeds, and knew this tree as *manele* or *a'e*.

KAMANI TREE

Calophyllum inophyllum

Kamani is a highly useful tree which was brought to Hawai'i by the early Polynesian voyagers. The sprawling tree, growing to a height of 60 feet, was widely cultivated in coastal areas. The hard, primarily reddish wood, was used for calabashes and other articles. *Kamani* also had important medicinal qualities. Today, the trees remain popular as ornamental shade trees prized for their salt tolerance, fragrant clusters of white flowers, and dark-green, highly durable leaves used for wreaths. Many more wood products are now made from kamani, but calabashes remain a favorite project.

WILIWILI TREE
Erythrina sandwicensis
Wiliwili

Wiliwili is a stout tree to 30 feet tall found from sea level to an elevation of 2,000 feet on the dry lee sides of all the main islands. It can thrive in the harsh, hot zones where many plants would suffer. The spreading, twisted limbs form a flat canopy bearing broad leaves and sprint flowers ranging in color from orange to white. A Hawaiian proverb claims that, when the *wili-wili* blooms, the sharks will bite. The light wood was used to make surf-boards, canoe outriggers, and net floats. An ancient grove of *wiliwili* may be seen by hiking into Koko Crater on O'ahu.

FLOWERING TREES

*F*ew things can compare with the magnificence of a towering tree, unless that tree is covered with beautiful blossoms. There are many trees in Hawai'i that are known for the spectacular show of flowers they possess. With our mild climate, trees of one sort or another are often in bloom through the year. Flowers are valued for their aesthetic qualities and fragrance, or simply because they are the tree's expression of love and symbolize the cycle and continuum of life. "Aloha" is, literally, "in the presence of the breath of life." Whether saying hello or goodbye, garlands of flowers, representing the circle of life, are given in the spirit of love. When a tree is blooming, we can reflect on this celebration of life's important activity of change and renewal.

PLUMERIA
Plumeria acuminata,
P. obtusa, P. rubra
Pua Melia

The fragrant and waxy flowers of this tropical American native greets the majority of the visitors to our islands in the form of floral garlands known as leis. The blossoms are borne in clusters on the ends of succulent stems, surrounded by rosettes of leaves. Colors of the flowers range from white to yellow and red to maroon, with many variations. Although the plant exudes a poisonous sap when wounded, its popularity has not been hindered by this fact. The trees are very drought-tolerant and thrive in hot, dry zones, where they are commonly cultivated. Horticulture is very simple and cuttings are easily rooted and grown. Outside of Hawai'i, this tree is more commonly known as frangipani.

CORAL TREE
Erythrina crista-galli

The twisted, sculptural limbs and corky bark of this Brazilian tree make it a popular choice of landscapers. It is of medium growth, rising to about 30 feet, with the added bonus of maroon-red blossoms putting on a display from December to April. Beautiful leis can be made with the flowers, but this is not commonly seen.

ERYTHRINA
Erythrina abyssinica

This African introduction is an open-crowned tree about 20 feet tall. The fissured bark and multiple thorns are offset by brilliant scarlet flowers held proudly like torches that bloom from the bottom up. It has an extended flowering season, with slowly opening inflorescences lasting from May to August. Following the blossoms are pods which resemble wooden beaded strands. The small, red seeds are often strung as leis in a striking spiral pattern.

AFRICAN TULIP TREE
Spathodea campanulata

The African tulip tree is most often seen in large public places that can accommodate its 70-foot, buttressed trunk. Its wind-dispersed seeds and its ability to readily germinate have allowed it to naturalize in many areas. The orange-red flowers are borne in rosette-like clusters and bloom sporadically through the year. A smaller form with beautiful, deep-yellow flowers is gaining popularity in landscapes. After blooming, stiff canoe-shaped pods emerge and split open to release the wind-borne seeds.

PINK TECOMA TREE
Tabebula pentaphylla

The pink tecoma is a tropical American tree widely valued because of its compact growth and attractive foliage, with the additional bonus of beautiful flowers that bloom occasionally throughout the year. Its ease of maintenance and tough nature make it a popular street tree.

ROSE FLOWERED JATROPHA
Jatropha hastata

This is a small-statured tree about 7 feet tall and native to Cuba. Superbly suited to hot, dry areas, its red blossoms welcome the heat of the tropical sun. The jatropha's resistance to drought makes it the perfect garden companion of succulents and cacti.

ROYAL POINCIANA
Delonix regia
'Ohai–'ula

Endangered in its homeland, Madagascar, the royal poinciana is very common and widely cultivated in Hawai'i. With sensuously twisted limbs, fin-like buttress roots, and a flat canopy crowned with ferny foliage, the mature trees exhibit great character. However, the trees are most famous for the spectacular show of color flaunted during the flowering season. The red-to-orange or yellow flowers may bloom in late winter, but the peak season is during June and July. The spent petals carpet the ground in red and orange hues following the all-out displays that completely cover the trees.

ROYAL POINCIANA

ROYAL POINCIANA

GOLD TREE

GOLD TREE
Tabebuia donnell-smithii

The majestic gold tree towers 75 feet or more at maturity. Native to Mexico and Central America, it is named for the spectacular flowering display that usually occurs in spring after the tree loses all of its leaves. The bell-shaped flowers are a brilliant yellow and bloom in spherical clusters. The blossoms soon fall to litter the ground with gold.

UMBRELLA TREE
Schefflera actinophylla

Umbrella trees are native to Australia, but are commonly seen in Hawai'i as house plants, landscape trees, and as escaped weeds on our hills. Once in the ground, they grow to a height of 40 feet, with sparse branching, open crowns, and aggressive roots. The name "umbrella tree" is derived from the palmate arrangement of the leaflets radiating out of a central axis like the spokes of an umbrella. This tree is also known as the "octopus tree," because of the multiple flower spikes that resemble the outstretched arms of the 6-foot cephalopod. The effect is heightened by the fact that the pink flowers and red, globose fruits resemble the suckers of a boiled, red octopus. Recently, the fruits have been strung into leis which are most often gifted to men.

RAINBOW SHOWER TREE
Cassia javanica X C. fistula

This common and popular landscaping tree is the resultant cross of a pink-and-white shower tree (*Cassia javanica*) with a golden shower tree (*Cassia fistula*). This hybrid produces copious blooms of peach-orange to red-blushed orange from March to August. The show of color is so magnificent that anyone witnessing the spectacle is left with a lasting impression. The dazzling effect is compounded by the liberal use of the trees in streets, parks, and on private properties throughout the State. Hawai'i has a substitute autumn, when the spent petals of the shower trees carpet the ground. Adding to its popularity, this hybrid rarely produces the messy and odiferous pods of the parent plants.

BOUGAINVILLEA
Bougainvillea spectabilis

The colorful bougainvillea is most commonly grown as a small shrub or untrimmed hedge or vine. The genus is named for Louis de Bougainville, who discovered it in Brazil. Rarely seen as trees in Hawai'i, the wild populations exhibit an elegant, upright form, with trunks up to 18 inches in diameter. The actual floral colors are borne by the bracts subtending the true flowers, which are nondescript and tubular. Bougainvillea has been popular in Hawai'i since its introduction around 1875, in spite of the strong thorns that protect the woody stems.

JACARANDA
Jacaranda mimosifolia

This popular tree, native to Northwestern Argentina and Bolivia, is widely grown in the cooler regions of Hawai'i. The bluish-purple flowers bloom over an extended period of time, but are particularly showy in early summer. The feathery foliage gives the trees a soft look. Somewhat rangy in growth at first, the trees become regal monarchs with age. In Brazil, the dark heartwood of jacaranda trees are valued for floors and furniture.

*I*t would be hard to determine if man prizes trees more for their wood or their fruit. The diversity of tropical fruits range from the familiar to the bizarre. The flavors are immediately loved, or slowly acquired, or abhorred—depending on the tastes of the diner. Sampling tropical fruits can be a wonderful adventure and the variety is almost endless. In Hawai'i, there are always special delights…here are a few fruits, common and rare, the visitor may encounter.

MOUNTAIN APPLE
Syzigium malaccense
'Ohi'a'ai

This Polynesian introduction is a native of the Malaysian forests and was used for food, wood, and medicine by the Hawaiians. The tree grows to 50 feet in wet forests at elevations of up to 1,800 feet. Tufts of red blossoms cling closely to the trunks of the trees in February to April. The flowers are short-lived and the spent blooms soon litter the forest floor with a scarlet carpet. Beginning in June, the succulent red fruits ripen and are eagerly sought for their sweet, refreshing flesh.

GUAVA
Psidium guajava

The guava, a tree native to the Neotropics, was introduced in the early 1800s by Don Francisco de Paula Marin. Today, it is widely cultivated and naturalized in Hawai'i, where it is considered a weed species. The sweet, pulpy fruit is used extensively for juice, jams, sorbet, and forms the basis of a minor agricultural crop. The abundant and easily dispersed seeds have spread the tree into the mountains, where their aggressive roots overpower many native species.

PAPAYA
Carica papaya

The papaya is a favorite breakfast fruit, and the small size and erect growth of the plants make it popular with home gardeners. Hawai'i also has a thriving commercial papaya industry with a seemingly endless demand. The exact history of papayas in Hawai'i is obscure, but it is generally thought that they arrived about the time of the first Western contact. Unbranched papaya trees superficially resemble palms, but often a few side branches develop on the tapering, hollow stalks. Plants can be male, female, or hermaphrodite. The fruits, usually eaten fresh, can be cooked, candied, or juiced. A popular Thai dish is green papaya salad, which contains the shredded raw flesh of immature fruits. The milky sap of the green fruits is used to isolate papain, a protein digestive useful in meat tenderizers and, recently, in spinal disc therapy.

STRAWBERRY GUAVA
Psidium cattleianum
Waiawi

The strawberry guava was probably introduced into Hawai'i by the HMS *Blonde* in 1825. Once here, this species became one of the most serious pests of the native forest due to its rampant growth and allelopathic qualities that prevent other plants from establishing around it. It was brought here for its excellent red fruit that is most often eaten fresh or in jams. The shapely trees are used extensively for landscaping, and old trees are very seductive with their beauty, but, like the sirens, they have a dark side to their charms.

MANGO
Mangifera indica

Mango is one of the most popular tropical fruits and it is often referred to as the "king of fruits." More than 500 varietal types are known in India alone. The dense shade and large size of mango trees has not diminished the planting of the trees in small Hawai'i yards. The sap of the plant, like its poison ivy relative, causes rashes of varying severity to susceptible people. Don Francisco de Paula Marin, who introduced several other premier fruits to Hawai'i, lays claim to the first planting of mango near Vineyard and River streets in downtown Honolulu. Over 40 horticultural varieties, including the most common Hayden and Pirie cultivars, were introduced later. The fruits are usually eaten fresh, dried, or pickled.

MANGO TREE

MANGO TREE

AVOCADO
Persea americana

The dean of Hawaiian fruit importers, Don Francisco de Paula Marin, planted the first local avocado trees in Pauoa, O'ahu. It was not until Wilson Popenoe propagated selected Fuerte variety budwood from Mexico in 1911 that superior grafted trees developed into the thriving avocado industry in the warmer United States. Worldwide annual production is several hundred thousand tons, which makes this a major agricultural crop. In 1935, the chance failure of a graft allowed the rootstock to grow, producing the leading, high-yield Hass clone. The large, rough-skinned fruits are prized for the buttery, oily flesh, high in carbohydrates and vitamins. The oil is extracted for soaps, cosmetics, and cooking.

BREADFRUIT
Artocarpus incisus

Breadfruit was a very useful tree in Polynesia, and the prehistoric voyagers to Hawai'i brought this plant with them. The wood made good, light canoe hulls, drums, and small household articles. The milky sap was used to caulk seams and as a sticky lime to snare birds. The bark was used as a source of fiber for tapa, although it was inferior to paper mulberry tapa. The large fruit was boiled, baked, steamed, or pounded into poi for eating. One or two trees could sustain a person through the year. The British had an interest in a cheap food source for their slaves on West Indian plantations when they sent Captain William Bligh, aboard the HMS *Bounty*, to gather breadfruit plants on Tahiti in 1788. Today, the trees remain popular in Hawai'i for their fruits and as striking ornamental shade trees.

JACKFRUIT
Artocarpus heterophyllus

This rare relative of the breadfruit, with dark-green, oval leaves, grows to 50 feet. The size of the fruits, which can measure three feet long and weigh 40 pounds, is impressive. The ripe fruit imparts an odor that many people find offensive, but, like durian, the pulp has a sweet, pleasant flavor. Due to the massive size of each fruit, however, an eating party must be organized just to consume one fruit from the prolific tree. The wood, which oxidizes from a blond to deep-brown color, makes wonderful furniture and would be a valuable timber tree.

MACADAMIA NUT
Macadamia integrifolia

The macadamia nut tree, a native of Australia, was introduced in Hawai'i by E. W. Purvis in 1885. Today, the culture and processing of macadamia nuts is a major industry for our state. The handsome, densely crowned tree bears copious amounts of nuts throughout the year. The reddish, close-grained wood is useful for cabinetry, but the nuts provide the greater economic yield for this tree.

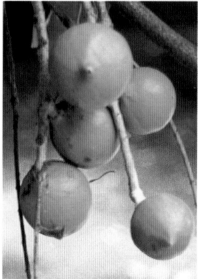

COFFEE
Coffea arabica

Coffee is a small tree to about 15 feet tall, but, to facilitate harvesting, is usually pruned to a low shrub. Only one crop of berries is produced each year, which starts a long process of harvesting, cleaning, drying, storing, roasting, and grinding. Don Francisco de Paula Marin brought the first plants to Hawai'i in 1813. Kona, on the Big Island, proved to be an ideal growing area and it has won international fame for its premier coffee.

STARFRUIT
Averrhoa carambola

The attractive evergreen leaves and medium growth to 20 feet tall make starfruit a popular backyard fruit tree. The fruits are borne two to three times a year, with large crops ripening all at once. The waxy fruits are five-angled and, when cross sectioned, form star-like perimeters. The watery pulp is acidic and sour in the pickling variety and a fragrant, sweet flesh distinguishes the eating variety. The immature fruits resemble leaves and blend into the foliage until they turn bright yellow upon ripening.

LYCHEE
Litchi chinensis

In 1852, lychee and other valuable oriental fruit trees were among the cargo of the ship carrying the first contract laborers from China to Hawai'i. The tree is prized for the small plum-sized fruit, which is covered by a rough, red skin. Over 200 pounds of the succulent fruit may be produced on the densely crowned tree. Canned and dried lychees are sold in many markets, but nothing compares with the sweet, delicate taste of the fresh fruits.

LYCHEE TREE

DATE PALM
Phoenix dactilifera

The date palm has a long history of cultivation with great importance in culture and religion. Christians introduced the Bible, as well as plants, to Hawai'i, with the missionary Edward Bailey credited for one of the first plantings of date palms in the 1850s. Palm Sunday was named in remembrance of the date fronds laid before the path of Jesus as he entered Jerusalem. Today, the fronds remain a symbol of martyrdom and victory. Although the date is not important economically in Hawai'i, there are about 800 uses recorded of the date palm ranging from food, to sugar production, to plaiting, and construction. In Hawai'i, the coconut is the preferred ornamental palm, especially since date palms must be manually trimmed of their thorny fronds to maintain a tidy appearance.

MAMMEE APPLE
Mammea americana

This large, tropical American tree, growing 30 to 60 feet tall, was introduced by the Scottish sea captain Alexander Adams in the 1800s. The woody fruit rind encloses a sweet, pear-like flesh that is eaten fresh or cooked. In its native homeland, the flowers, sap, and fruit are used to make refreshing drinks. The gum and seeds are used insecticidally, and the leaves treat fever. The hard, brown wood is used for posts and other construction. The mammee apple on the grounds of the State's Department of Agriculture on King and Keeaumoku Streets is one of the best examples of this tree in the United States.

DURIAN TREE
Durio zibethinus

King Kalakaua is credited with introducing this tree in 1881, after his world tour. A few seeds of this forest giant, originally from Borneo and famous for the fruits which smell like the sewer but taste like the finest French custard, were planted. The spiky, football-sized fruit is widely cultivated in Southeastern Asia for the delicious fruit, but the smell bans it from many public places such as hotels and airplane cabins. There are many descriptions of the smell which usually follow along the lines of bathroom odors or dead animals. This smell is long lasting and some diners burp as a side effect of the indulgence. The glorious pulp is so highly prized among connoisseurs that durian parties are held so that the scent can be shared. Like other important fruits, many select clones are recognized for durian with names like, "Transvestite," for a form with soft flesh and no seeds. For all its popularity in Asia, durian remains rare in Hawai'i, the only suitable place in the United States to grow this tender, tropical tree that can reach heights of 100 feet.

ORANGE TREE

ORANGE TREE
Citrus sinensis

About eleven species of citrus are native to Southeast Asia. When Western explorers began their extended sea voyages, every effort was made to introduce citrus trees for the purpose of reprovisioning at various landfalls. Scurvy was debilitating to men long at sea and the ascorbic acid in citrus was necessary to control the ailment. Calling a sailor "limey" arose from this practice of feeding limes and other citrus to British seamen. Achibald Menzies, surgeon and naturalist on Captain George Vancouver's ship *Discovery*, introduced the first orange trees to Hawai'i in 1792. One of the original trees still grows in Kona on the Big Island.

TAMARIND TREE
Tamarindus indica
Wi'awa'awa

Tamarind, famous in Indian cuisine, is native to the dry regions of Asia and tropical Africa. The pods provide a sour pulp that is prized as an ingredient for curries, chutneys, soups, and drinks. The name tamarind is Latinized from an Arabic word meaning "Indian date." The tree has been very important to Asian culture. It has been used for dyes, medicines, and timber. The beautiful tan wood is very durable and prized for furniture. In Hawai'i, the primary use is as a landscape shade tree in the hot areas where it thrives. Don Francisco de Paula Marin, who introduced guava, is credited with planting the first tamarind tree on Fort Street in Honolulu in 1797.

TAMARIND TREE

ORNAMENTAL TREES

*T*here is no measure for the gratitude of shade, nor is there an objective scale for beauty that will accommodate all tastes. This section presents a range of introduced trees and simply celebrates trees in their myriad of forms. These species are easily seen by the visitor to Hawai'i, and loving a tree for its own sake is an intrinsically spiritual experience.

BE-STILL TREE
Cascabela thevetia

This beautiful and common ornamental plant is also deathly poisonous, as the name "be still" implies. The sap of all parts contains thevetin, a strong heart depressant. It is most often used in hedges and as street plantings. The dense, fine-textured foliage is lime-green and punctuated throughout the year by bright-yellow, tubular flowers. The genus name *Cascabela* refers to the small, bell-shaped fruits of the plant. It has been cultivated in Hawai'i since the turn of the century.

MONKEYPOD
Samanea saman

Native to the Neotropical region from Mexico to Brazil, the monkeypod was introduced into Hawai'i about 1871. In its place of origin, it is known as the "raintree," due to the fact that "rain" constantly falls from the canopy. It has been discovered that this phenomenon is caused by the excretions of cicadas. Luckily, Hawai'i does not have cicadas and the monkeypod, up to 80 feet tall, with its beautiful, symmetrical crown, is a favorite shade tree. The beautiful wood is easily worked and many articles are made from this tree.

MONKEYPOD

MONKEYPOD

CHRISTMAS BERRY
Schinus terebinthifolius
Wilelaiki

Many wreaths are made in the fall from the red, clustered fruits of the Christmas berry tree. The highly ornamental tree, with its furrowed bark and twisted form, makes a beautiful landscape specimen. The copious red fruit of the female trees is easily dispersed, and the Christmas berry has become a naturalized pest, forming great thickets. Once established in a wild area, the allelopathic roots of the Christmas berry inhibit the growth of other plants, adding to its noxious character. The name "wilelaiki" is derived from the politician, Willie Rice, who often wore a hat lei made of the red berries.

LIPSTICK PLANT
Bixa orellana
'Alaea

The lipstick plant is a small tree grown for its prickly fruit capsules, which are often seen in dry flower arrangements. The scarlet coating over the numerous seeds yielded a tasteless yellow dye useful in food colorings before the appearance of synthetic substitutes. The red seed coat gave the lipstick plant its common name. *'Alaea* means "Ocherous earth" and refers to the yellow dye. It escaped cultivation and became naturalized in Nu'uanu Valley, O'ahu, by 1865.

BEACH HELIOTROPE
Tournefortia argentea

This common beach tree is native to tropical Asia through Polynesia, but is considered an introduced species in Hawai'i, first reported on O'ahu in 1864 or 1865. It is a highly useful landscape tree in windy, salty, and dry areas of the coast. Very ornamental, the beach heliotrope becomes increasingly elegant with age. The corky bark and sensuous branches are crowned by succulent, light-green leaves which provide cooling shade on hot sands.

KOU HAOLE
Cordia sebestena

This small tree is most often seen as a street tree in the dry lowland. The dark-green leaves, neat canopy, small stature, and year-round blooming of orange blossoms add to its desirability. The dark heartwood is sometimes made into small items and many parts of the tree are said to be medicinal.

SILK OAK
Grevillea robusta
Haʻiku keʻokeʻo

Introduced into Hawaiʻi in 1880, this native of Eastern Australia has naturalized here largely due to reforestation programs. Between 1919 and 1959, over 2.2 million trees were planted for timber. The valuable wood has a beautiful checkered grain and superior structure. Very few trees are harvested in Hawaiʻi, and the dust created during milling is harmful to breathe. The common name is derived from the oak-like wood and the silver, silky look of the ferny foliage. The tree is used in landscaping hot, dry areas and grows quickly to heights of 100 feet. From May to July, the attractive orange flowers bloom in upright clusters 3 to 4 inches long.

FALSE KAMANI
Terminalia catappa
Kamani haole

This native of Malaysia is a large, ornamental tree adapted to life along the coast. It is grown for shade, wood, dyes, and medicine. Its edible nuts, eaten raw or roasted, give the tree its other common name— "tropical almond." The branches are held out horizontally and arranged in tiers, which makes this tree easy to identify. The large, oval leaves are long lasting and turn bright red before finally falling. The foliage is not shed all at once, so the tree appears to be evergreen. The hard, reddish wood is very durable and used for boat and house construction.

INDIAN BANYAN
Ficus benghalensis

The banyan derived its name from Hindu traders who cherished the tree. Hindus also considered the banyan sacred and it became one of the symbols of the Cosmic Tree of Life. With great age, the banyan attains incredible proportions. One tree is claimed to have covered an area of 2,000 feet in circumference, providing shade for as many as 20,000 people under its 100-foot-tall canopy. Over 3,000 aerial or prop roots helped to support the giant tree, which truly ranks as one of nature's miracles.

CHINESE BANYAN
Ficus microcarpa

This large tree, which originated in Southeast Asia, has naturalized in many parts of Hawai'i. There is a wonderful avenue of this banyan species in Hilo on the Big Island. Forty-five notable personalities, including Franklin Delano Roosevelt, Amelia Earhart, and Babe Ruth, planted this unique avenue. The tunnel created by the massive trees and the curtains of slender aerial roots add up to a theatrical effect well worth visiting.

NORFOLK ISLAND PINE
Araucaria heterophylla

Araucaria trees are considered to be of ancient lineage and the family used to be one of the most widespread of the seed-bearing plants during the Mesozoic era. Arizona's Petrified Forest is dominated by fossil trunks of Araucaria and attests to the past abundance of these conifers. Today, the family is restricted in its native distribution, but the popularity of the trees for reforestation projects has seen its introduction to all corners of the globe. The Norfolk island pine is often grown as a small container plant. The fact that they can attain a height of 170 feet has not deterred owners of small properties from planting their own Christmas tree. The blond wood encircled by dark knot wood is commonly used to turn bowls or to make veneer and paneling.

SWAMP MAHOGANY
Eucalyptus robusta

Introduced to Hawai'i in the 1880s, the swamp mahogany is now the most abundantly planted timber tree in the Islands. Nearly 5 million trees were planted by 1960. The deeply furrowed bark distinguishes this tall tree that grows rapidly to about 100 feet. The famous tree tunnel on Kaua'i is an avenue planted with this species. Although heavily damaged by Hurricane Iniki, the trees are recovering, and the drive on Maluhia Road to Koloa town is highly recommended.

MINDANAO GUM
Eucalyptus deglupta

The Mindanao gum is native to the Southern Philippines down to Papua, New Guinea, and thus is one of the few non-Australian species of eucalyptus. It is considered to be the seventh tallest tree species in the world, attaining heights up to 200 feet. Harold L. Lyon imported the first seeds of Mindanao gum in 1939 from New Guinea. The most remarkable characteristic of this tree is the multi-hued swatches of color that "paint" the satiny trunk with greens, blues, lavenders, and browns with reddish tones. The painted look is a masterpiece of natural abstraction that is everchanging as the bark peels off layers.

IRONWOOD
Casuarina equisetifolia

Ironwoods were introduced to Hawai'i about 110 years ago. The trees grow well near the ocean and are very common on the beach up to the high-water line. The genus Casuarina is derived from the slender, tufted needles that resemble cassowary feathers (*Casaurius*). The species name, *equisetifolia*, comes from the similarity of the foliage to horsetail rushes (*Equisetium*). The ironwood makes an excellent windbreak, but the aggressive roots prevent almost all other plants from growing near them. The dense, red wood is a good fuel and, like its common name, hard as iron.

TRAVELER'S PALM
Ravenala madagascariensis

Traveler's palms are not palms but are related to bananas. They hold a large reserve of water in their leaf bases from which travelers could drink. It would be a mighty desperate soul to partake of the stagnant, insect- and debris-laden cocktail contained in this traveler's "oasis." The distinctive, flat fan formed by the leaves and leaf bases makes the traveler's palm a popular and unique ornamental. The plants grow very rapidly to 30 feet and more.

RHAPIS PALM
Rhapis excelsa

This palm, commonly known also as the lady or bamboo palm, is very useful in landscaping as a hedge planting or specimen clump. The thin, cane-like stems and dark-green palmate foliage are easily maintained and provide a neat appearance to the areas in which they are grown. Many plants are also used in interior plantings, which attests to their adaptability. Although they can attain a height of 12 feet, they are most often seen as smaller plants. There are many clones and varieties of this palm, which is so highly valued in Japan that certain types are traded on a central exchange like stocks.

MAHOGANY
Swietenia mahogoni

The dense, close-grained hardwood of mahogany trees is one of the most valuable lumbers in the world. It was reserved to make many of the premier furniture, cabinets, and musical instruments. In Hawai'i, the trees are planted for shade and for reforestation species. The trees can reach a height of 75 feet, with trunks 5 feet in diameter.

SAUSAGE TREE
Kigelia pinnata

Native to tropical Africa, the sacred sausage tree is well named for its odd, pendant fruits. The tree forms a graceful canopy, but the sight of sausages hanging from long stems creates a comic atmosphere around this plant. The inedible fruits may be as much as 3 feet long and weigh 15 pounds apiece. The large, velvety, maroon flowers are night blooming, foul scented, and bat pollinated, which befits this improbable tree.

PAPERBARK
Melaleuca leucodendron

Paperbark, native to the region from Australia and Southeast Asia, is named for the white, spongy bark which can be peeled off in sheets. The trees have been used extensively in Hawai'i for reforestation and city landscaping. The durable wood is used for fuel, posts, and shipbuilding. Aromatic oil which has several medicinal applications can be expressed from the leaves.

PAPERBARK

EARPOD TREE
Enterolobium cyclocarpum

The earpod tree is named after the distinctive dark pods which assume flat, ear-like shapes. It is a 100-foot giant with a broad spread to its canopy. Earpods are native to a wide area of the Neotropics from Mexico to Brazil. Dr. William Hillebrand planted an example of this species in the 1850s to fulfill his interest in introducing timber trees useful for shipbuilding and repair. The tree may still be seen in Foster Botanical Gardens, as Hillebrand's property is now known.